T0209748

SONNETS
FROM THE
NEW WORLD

DAVID GEORGE

EDITED BY LISA A. LARRABEE

authorHOUSE®

AuthorHouse™
1663 Liberty Drive
Bloomington, IN 47403
www.authorhouse.com
Phone: 1 (800) 839-8640

Published by AuthorHouse 09/23/2019

ISBN: 978-1-7283-2431-9 (sc)
ISBN: 978-1-7283-2430-2 (e)

Print information available on the last page.

This book is printed on acid-free paper.

Dedicated to

the Blessed Virgin Mary

INTRODUCTION

by David George

I usually recommend that you let the poetry speak for itself.

CONTENTS

VI. NIGHTS OF WOODSMOKE

VII. SIGHTING REALITY THROUGH
THE NECK OF A BOTTLE

VIII. SOONER OR LATER DELICATE DEATH

IX.   THE MAN WHO WENT BEYOND E=MC2

X.   GALAXIES

I.

THE SHAPE OF THINGS

THE SHAPE OF THINGS

The ever-expanding curve of things to come
Began to move before the earth was born.
It arches over everything. Each line
Bends to fit the apex of where it has been,
And stretches into what it will become.

The shapes of things determine what they are:
Perfect spheres of falling water fall
In shapes that never vary from the norm;
A circle is born when air and water form
Mute alliance within a molecule.

Soul is circle. How could it be square?
Towers lean, but circles float in air.
And tons of snowflakes, falling on a pond,
Become, in fact, what they are falling on.

EDWARD HOPPER'S ROOM IN BROOKLYN (1932)

A vase a lamp a chair in a room in Brooklyn—
Metamorphosed by the language of light—
Once were objects in the bright dimension
Of a painter's mind.

                 What arcane trait
Set Hopper apart from the drift of the world-at-large?
What ever-expanding light made him energize
The properties of common things, and charge
The ordinary with greatness?

                    Under the guise
Of vase and lamp and chair, he left it bare—
Illuminated by a light that fell
Enamel-white upon a windowsill.

And objects bright beyond a gilded frame,
Beyond a room in Brooklyn, beyond his time,
Transfigured light until they became monumental.

RAINBOW

I saw a rainbow lift out of water and leap
Back into its origins.
                    In one vast arc,
It cast a light that curved in falling back,
As if the sky were speaking to the deep
In mystical remarks.
                    It spoke of hope:
The bright unraveling of what is bound
Between the flowing river and the ground.

It spoke of things that swim in myth and sleep—
Things rarely seen, things that began before
A rainbow came to illuminate in mist
The darker patterns of a valley floor.

I stood transfixed—a shadow in the grass—
Thinking the thoughts of a child in a candy store
Who spends his penny on splendor and stained glass.

HOUSE BY A RAILROAD

A watercolor by Charles Burchfield

In this painting, the road doesn't go anywhere.
A slice of it slides by—a slab of grey—
Stops at the corner, and disappears into sky

As if it wasn't meant to stay somewhere,
As if it were destined for a larger space—
The far reaches—where roads go twisting away.

Nothing about this day is ordinary:
A house is there, with a slanted roof and the stare
Some old houses have on the edge of nowhere,
And sun glints off a broken windowpane.

There is no train or track. A crossing sign,
Riddled with bullets, stands in its own design—
Stark against thistles and mustard wild in the sun.
And that is all. No people. Nothing but sun.

THE MAN IN THE MARBLE PIT AT CARRARA

Deep in a pit, he hacked away at stone
As if his life depended upon each stroke.
A dozen blows, and then he paused, stepped back,
Shaking his head like a man will with a woman.

What he saw in it, nothing before him had seen—
Assuming the sun, the eyes of a high-flying hawk,
Were not drawn to the meaning in that rock—
Naked and plain on the surface of its skin
But dark to the bone.
                              Yet what he saw within
The twisted grain and contour of that block—
What giants strode there, what half-frozen face
Stared back at him with the glazed, inspired look
Of his own frenzied gaze, he didn't say.
Nor did he speak of the gargoyles that lurk in the dark.

FLIGHT-PATH

The bird against my window in the dark
Hit with a thud, like a thrown clod of earth,
But with a darker sound.

                            The click of its beak
Punctuated its passing, its last breath—
All it had time for, before a bone-breaking shock
Bounced it off and down to the kind of death
It didn't expect from such a routine flight.

Even when frost paints my window white, they hit.
Like moths, or June-bugs, mesmerized by light,
They just can't seem to re-align their sights
From what this was before it was a house.

Each time they hit, I wonder if its right
To squat where birds believe the sky is theirs—
And if, in fact, the sky is meant to be shared.

REFLECTIONS ON A
SHAPELY FORM IN FLIGHT

"In order for there to be a mirror of the world
it is necessary that the world have a form."
—Umberto Ecco, *The Name of the Rose*

What if the world were formless—what would there be
To shine upon itself, shape meaning, sight?
What is light without shadows to reflect—
Look back upon, regret?

                         Nothing but sky—
An abstract emptiness. Reality
Needs a fact to demonstrate a fact:
The bee, the flower, the moving silhouette—
A hawk alighting in a barren tree
Mirrors, in light rays, what a hawk can be.

Thinking of these things, I cast a stone
Skipping over the surface of a pond.
The stone transformed in flight—

                         the stone became
A silver disk that skittered before it fell
Into a dim reflection of itself.

BEAUTY

Sometimes unexpectedly, unbidden,
Beauty comes. Not a downpouring of doves,
Not a Venus, sheathed in an ivory shell,
Not even the lenses of Stonehenge in its season—
Stones aligned to catch the sun as it moves
Mystically, majestically, through holes
And crevices.

           Not even these spectaculars—
The light against the dark, the white ecstatic,
Stars falling and setting the sky on fire—
Take possession, or let the moment take
The horse high over the hedge with an unseen rider.

It comes when least expected, when the dark
Opens a crack to let light filter in—
A word, a look, a sudden realization.

FROM THE NOTEBOOKS OF JOHN THE ALCHEMIST

"When I pored over these old texts,
Everything fell into place."
—C.G. Jung, *Memories, Dreams, Reflections*

Dark of aspect, behind its sullen mask
The unknown force that passes through the glass
Is still anonymous, still puts on the face
Of twisted innocence.

                  I dare not ask
Questions of dark intent, nor do I peer
Deeply into the mist behind the mask.
The risk is worth the taking, but it's a risk—
Solve et coagula—

               as when I poured
Excelsior into the beaker, and bits of quartz
Hissed in the crystal, coagulated, invoked
A force so stark in its smoky explosiveness

I backed off, afraid to find in its place
The shape of a smirking, darkly sardonic face—
Fragments of eyes staring back in the shattered glass.

STONE

Stone has so deep a sense of its certainty,
It seems to sleep when others lie awake
Staring like owls, because they cannot speak
Of what they cannot see.

                    Stone doesn't try
To scale a height, or sail a glassy sea
To touch eternity's face the mask
Ullyses wore, or Icarus,

                    nor does it ask
Why it is lying so quietly in its shell,
Nor does it seem aware of other souls
Stirring in space beyond its molecules.

Stone stands still in the pool of its solitude—
In striking contrast to that immortal clay
Shifting indecisively, with mind and eye
Only half open, and still unsychronized.

II.

THINGS OF THE SEA
BELONG TO THE SEA

THINGS OF THE SEA
BELONG TO THE SEA

The shell in my hand, no bigger than my fist,
Is closing down because it must exist.

Hinged like a drawbridge, its embattled gate
Guards the glow of its inner ornament—
The ghost of the oyster that activates the pearl—
The soul within, the world without the pale.

I run my fingers over its grooves and scars
Encrusted with lichen and barnacle and weed—
Medals won in combat, the outer war
It wages with the sea.
                                    I feel the tide
Surge around my ankles—on every side
Suction, pressure, a tugging intensity
Heightened by the grip of what I hold in my hand,
Surrender gently, and step back up on land.

THE BIRTH OF VENUS

When she was born, a wind was in the waves.
They crested high and white, as if the ocean
Felt the impact of something going on,
Something bright in the deep of its dark cave.

Trumpets blared. The mainsprings of their valves
Unleashed the yellow sound of another sun—
The one behind the eye, behind the shine
That radiated through her many lives.

What thing occurred, cried out, and then lay still
Upon the water in its womb of brine?
Pristine in spite of its passage through the green,

She must have been more than beauty, more than a pearl,
More than the freestanding figure of a woman
That Botticelli painted upon a shell.

THE SEA IS WAITING,
LIKE PENELOPE

The sea is turning over under its breath
The broken bones of shells and sea-struck men
Who went to sleep with the taste of sand in their mouth.

The sea leans back and weaves a tapestry
Of green and weedy tide, a tattered shroud
Of intricate brocade.
                    The ships of Troy
Still adrift in the myth of a stony sea,
Shift in their sandy caskets, and sailors say:
"Let's go down in ships to where they lie,
Let's dredge a sea-bed deeper than history."

The sea says nothing. It rolls in the wind and weeps.
The wife on the widow-walk understands the sea.
She knows the mist, the sting of salt on her face.
They both have reasons to be weary and deep.

JACK-SALMON

I caught a salmon whose wings were severed, and fins
Grew out of its backbone. I caught it leaping upstream
To spawn. I caught it on a silver spoon,
And netted it half in water and half in dream—
Its body arched and curving away from me,
Still swimming east.

                "That's a big Jack, buddy."
The guy on the left was leaning over to look.
"Torn up some, but there's still plenty to smoke."

And then I was a salmon, back in the bay,
Fresh from the sea, and running upstream to spawn,
Feeling the fight and the color go out of me.

As dawn turned to day, and the day was drained of its light,
I was still leaping barriers—rock over rock—
Leaping, leaping, still leaping in spite of the hook.

THE SPIDER-CRAB

A spindly spider-crab with spokes for legs
Walks out upon the rocks I'm standing on.

Not far below, the tide is coming in—
A shapeless thing that surges, lingers, sags,

Climbs higher in a swirl of foam that marks
The sun-baked rocks with the dark of its design—
The same uncertain deck I'm standing on.

The spider-crab seems unconcerned with the sea,
Steps stiffly out upon a shifting rock—
A hunter stalking what a hunter seeks.

The sea explodes with spray where the spider stood,
And washes down a web of shell and weed.

The rocks are wet and gleaming in the sun
But suddenly empty, now that the spider's gone.

WHALE-WATCHING FROM AN OPEN BOAT

Their rising always comes as a surprise.

The sea is calm, and then a whale appears—
Breaks surface, waves awash in its wake.
The mist of its blowhole drifts away, as it sucks
Fresh air in.
                  In spite of the surf, I can hear
The suffing sound of its breathing as it blows.
I'm close enough to see how drops of water
Cling like pearls in the ridges of its eyes.

I study whales. Perhaps they study me.
I sense they need the vast immensities
Of open sea, unbroken distances

To think about, to sing their mournful songs in—
Even as I, by watching them, transcend
The cluttered canyons my intelligence moves in.

THE TURTLE

The turtle shell lay gaping in the sand.
Inverted like a bowl, or a small boat,
And peeled by the sea down to its outer coat,
It once enclosed a turtle-soul that spawned
A turtle-body that swam and waddled on land.

But now the turtle, ragged and remote,
Lay naked on a crest of sand apart.
Far from the weedy crash of tide, it lay stranded
Where the last high wave abandoned it.

I came upon this echo of a turtle
While walking a beach where gulls were loud in the sun.
Schools of dolphin were leaping in white swells,
And all was alive and well, except for one—
Nothing but shadow in an empty shell.

BEYOND THE BEACH

Beyond the beach, where waves are laced with weed,
The broken walls of sunken cities stand
In blue exile.
                    What did they call this land
That sank beneath a sudden rush of tide?
Fish are feeding where a temple stood.

On marble altars, deep in shell and sand,
Dolphins are carved in black obsidian.
Where are the street-signs, where are those who died
Reaching for each other in the tide?

Now divers sift through skull and scattered bone
Searching in silence for gold and silver coin.
They do not care whose bones are in the mud,
Whose blood is in the briny of the sea—

Nor do the fish, feeding on green jade.

SEAWARD LEANS THE SHELL

Seaward leans the shell upon the land.
The tines of its fluted porcelain are bent
Toward the listing waves of its lament.
Gleaming with seawash, and salty in its span,
I hold this small dark chalice in my hand
As if the sea were riding in its spell,
As if this shell were more than empty shell
That I found tilting seaward in the sand.

Was it cast by accident or design
To look like a white hand reaching for the sea?
Perhaps there is more to mother-of-pearl than meets
The outer eye. Perhaps each particle,
Even dead barnacles on the backs of whales
Are part of the broken riddle of water and light.

THE DOLPHIN

To know the ocean as a dolphin does—
The easy motion of gliding through a wave
And out the other side, as if it has
Intuitive understanding of the laws
That govern surge and flow,

                         the dolphin has
Refined itself. Nothing can slow its graceful
Slide through a running tide—its fins and tail
Send it surging into the wave's caress.

The dolphin is so intimate with surf
That each small wave, even the sea itself,
Glides within the green of a dolphin's brain.

It moves as the sea moves, rides each windy swell,
Leaps with the sea-bright skill of a dancer, until
The dance of dolphin and the wave are one.

FOUND-OBJECT

Tangled in seaweed, it glittered like a shell
That looked the worse for wear in that green thicket.

I picked it up and put it in my pocket
Because I wanted something impractical—
An afterthought, a little piece of bell
To jingle when I later took it out.

The knack of it eluded me. I thought
The simple act of possession would cast a spell,
Carry me out like driftwood in the tide
And cast me back alive with the thrill of it.

Not so. It had the look of porcelain—
Pocked and pitted—as if a dream had died,
As if the sea, in polishing that bone,
Had done the best with beauty that it could.

III.

IN THE BEGINNING IS THE UGLY

IN THE BEGINNING
IS THE UGLY

Not ugly because it is toadlike, only because
In the beginning of everything is the ugly:
The tadpole, the duckling, the frog before it is princely—
Dragons that grin with pink and pearly jaws.

The harsh incongruity of stark surprise
Flusters, shocks, delays receptivity.
The news is lost: the beauty behind the ugly,
Behind the look.
     The beauty I speak of defies
Analysis. It lies about things of the earth.
The bent bamboo, the drumbeat, the sucked-in breath
Come closer to definition than the word.

But who's to say what keyhole in the sky
Was cut to fit the eye that spies on God?
I listen to fish because they live in the sea.

THE SCULPTOR

Once he sensed what in the stone was his
And what was not and what was laid in the grain,
He walked around until he saw the shape
Of things unseen.

                    What harsh impersonal press
Of sun and wind upon the inert stone
Had left its mark in flowers and in scars?

He took up chisel and chiseled to the bone
Until the bare stone opened under his hand,
Until it came to life under his breath.

A head appeared, a torso, and then a man
Pre-empted space that was barren and empty before
The hand of the sculptor descended upon the other,

Before the myth of nothingness and death
Was tested by the closed fist of the sculptor.

FROM A FOOTNOTE IN THE BOOK OF THE DEAD

If all beginnings begin in the back of the mind
He was in darkness, groping for the word
To start it up—for there was nothing but void.

Imagine the void: A clear light, undefined—
No name to utter, no form for the eye to find,
Just a veiled footnote in the Book of the Dead
Barely translatable.
                              Yet he uncoiled
A blinding force in the briny tongue of the wind
That wet down everything. It took a mind
Darker than star, a brighter wheel than sun
To start it up—

                              to mingle inspired spittle
With common clay, with ecstasy, with light—
Until it fanned the spark of a sudden thought
That struck fire, and brought the world about.

STAINED-GLASS IN A CRYSTAL PARADISE

Like smoke and cloud, opaque but delicate,
They interchanged in thought and attitude
Untouched transparencies.

                      Alike in mood,
They understood the misting of the light
That left their flesh in shadows at their feet.
There was no night, no death; ingratitude
Had not been invented yet.

                      What did they do
To occupy the intervals between
Fruit and flower, the wave's caress, the flow
Reflected in the even glow of sun
Upon their skin?

                It strains the imagination
To think of them alone in infinite space—
Lightly attired, and stepping gently around
The green-eyed gardener dozing in the grass.

THINKING ABOUT WILD GEESE GOING OVER

I do not think wild geese intend to cast
Reflections on still water, nor does the water
Intend to bend these images still further,
Unless the mind of water reflects its past—
If water has a mind of its own.

                        When last
Released, it seemed to brood. Behind its breath
A mind began to move with a steady stealth
Of wind rising, and rain,

                      and then a blast
That made a sea of sky and land, until
The wild geese going over had no place
To rest.

        Perhaps the geese, like mind itself,
Are superimposed upon a concept of space
Where nothing in time is missing or amiss—
And water exists to darkly reflect the geese.

THOUGHTS IN THE SISTINE CHAPEL

There, on the ceiling, God's finger reaching out
Nearly touches Adam's finger, yet
Why the distance? Why did he hesitate?

In that instant, it came to me in a flash:
Geometry, Epistomology—
The folding and unfolding of the flesh
As things pile up in the backwash of the sea.

In that instant, a narwhale came to rest.
A dinosaur unfurled its length of bone.
I saw a cathedral rise out of the ribs of a beast
That would, in time, give birth to another one.

Nothing is impossible. The least is most.
And most of all are the swallows that perch on stone—
Build their nests, and nestle bone to bone.

UNDER THE JESSE WINDOW
IN CHARTRES CATHEDRAL

Out of the Rod of Jesse, springs a tree
With amethyst leaves, and limbs of the darkest jade.

Rooted in topaz, its jasper trunk was made
Stone-hard and stark.

                        No drift-wood on the sea,
No sacred oak, was fashioned as cunningly
As this deliberate act of a crafty god

Who let the hand of art convert plain glass
Into a crystal, inlaid with garnets and rubies—
The bloodless ice of celestial sacrifice.

What radiant thing reclines at the summit of life?
It shines in the truth of its tower, a starry sphere
Permeated and ripe,

                    like a pomegranate
Scattering seeds that burst through the skin of its coat
To root in the shadow of light-rays, and bear fruit.

THE DOME

His voice flares out in a dome of many voices—
Banked choirs of bells, chimes in the void—
The burning meditations of genesis
Turn in the yearning of a lonely lord.

At first he counted the darkness under his breath:
One, he said, and there was light. Two, he said,
And it began to rain.
                            He made the earth
Flower at dawn to decorate the day,
And then leaned back to admire what he had made.

What thing is there that weathers beyond birth,
That flows and flowers even after death?
Or is he alone in a barren landscape of bones—
Doomed to cry out in the dome of his loneliness,
Always alone among the echoing angels?

A TIME FOR SOARING AND FOR FALLING BACK

I saw a star that fell into the dark:
A blaze of light, and then it was no more—
As if in the soaring it had lost its spark,
Fell back upon the undemanding air.

So it is with soaring, the falling back
Upon a place where dark and endless space
Cools the ardor, like a star that takes
Time to fall beyond the fire-place.

The floor of the valley is littered with meteors
That blazed for an instant and fell into the deep
Of what they were.
                    So it is with the warrior
That burns with a holy fire, the child in sleep,
The lady in black, the bride on the widow's walk,
The man in grey who meets himself coming back.

AQUARIUMS

Aquariums begin with panes of glass
Tightly fitted to keep the water in.
Then come sand, and pebbles, and colored stone—
Snails and shells, and rocks with crevices
For the fish to hide in.
                     And weeds, of course—
Vertical weeds that break the surface, and weeds
That merely float, and lights that emphasize
Bulging fish eyes, magnified by glass,
That push against and peer through barriers.

This is how aquariums begin.
This is how it all began—the sky,
The sea, the first breath of anything that is—
Beginning with the mind behind the eye
That loves like light what it illuminates.

IV.

A SENSE OF ORDER IN ANOTHER ARENA

A SENSE OF ORDER IN ANOTHER ARENA

They put their sense of it in the lion's mouth
Directly, without pretense or ceremony
Masking the fact of the stance they chose to assume.

For they, only they—not the Truth, not the Light, not
                                        the Way—
Defined in a public act their destiny,
As they went singing into the lion's mouth.

I'm sure a hush descended upon the crowd—
One of those rare, historic hushes when
Even the drunken among us can sense an event—
Even the scholar, the dancing theologian.

Then, as at a bullfight, the sands must be swept—
Water-carts come out to keep down the dust—
The carnage cleared away, the lions led
Gently, carefully, back to their stone cages.

CHAPELS AND TABERNACLES

"Alone and warming his five wits,
"The white owl in the belfrey sits."
—Tennyson

Six monks in cowls, robes white against the snow,
Go single file beneath a Great White Owl
That calmly watches from its cubicle.

Six monks at dawn go out upon the world
To exercise, to contemplate, to know
God in his moods as well as in his word—
They stride with solemn purpose through the snow.

Had they looked up at the gargoyle looking down—
The owl of rude and sweeping wing that rides
The night-air knowingly,

would they have seen
Reflections of their own ravenous souls
Red and gold in the hollows of its eyes?

Or does each monk, in the forest of his mind,
Dismiss what he sees as only wilderness?

WHAT THE DESERT FATHER SAID

Where dust is, God is, The Desert Father said:
The dust of dawn, the dust in the mouth of the dead,
And what I do with my dust.
                                    From smoke and birdflight,
From blood-stains dark on the fragile bones of a lizard,
Comes solar-dust—the soul of a fallen star—
Changing texture in the diminished light
Of wind-driven sand that swirls in the desert air.

I must have been flecked from birth with a layer of dust
That rearranges intricate molecules
Whenever I take a step, whenever I stop,
Whenever I stride through dust-pools out of the past.

And if I jar even so much as a pebble,
The stars are not responsible, or heaven—
Not even the ghost that scribbles its name in the dust.

UNLESS A MAN BE BORN
AGAIN FROM ABOVE

Born again from above, not from below—
The worms complaining bitterly under the snow:
Where has he gone? Where is he now? They grieve.

A snail ascending, he walked away from his shell—
Left it standing coiled, a small cathedral
Empty, hollow, not even the sound of a footfall
Loud on the tile,

                    not even a glimpse of the soul
That spiraled him into spark, the compelling force
That cast him loose at the breathing instant of birth
And took him back breathless at the hour of death,

Not even a drop for those greedy animals
Who grope in the towering hollow of a bone
Like Easter Sunday at the altar rail . . .

They will find nothing, not even a particle.

THAT BUILDING IN NEW YORK

What building is this with lions on a ledge—
Crouching in space, like a testy lioness
Caught in the flow of an unfamiliar place?

Who cast these shapes? Are they of another age?
Are these the lions that roar upon a stage
Where sand and sky converge upon the soul?
Wild or tame, are they imperial?

These questions linger—like lions on a ledge
That seem to doze in the cages of their eyes.
The sandstone of their skin reflects the sun
That touches with its tongue each tawny mane
Until it seems to ripple in response.

How long will the sun glaze over their stone eyes
Before they arise, angry and ravenous?

TO MOVE IN TIME BEYOND THE METRONOME

"But such a form as Grecian goldsmiths make
Of hammered gold and gold enameling"
—W.B. Yeats, "Sailing to Byzantium"

The black and white inside the metronome
Are breaking against the stained-glass of their cage.
Ink wells up and colors the modern age:
The lithographic font, the four colors of time,
Are skillfully laid in images that rhyme.

Is this a song? A sonnet carved in rock?
The silent reader is rowing stroke by stroke
Across the silence of what the sea has become.
Who is that figure standing on the shore?
It moves in dream. It moves in the dark like a dancer.

The show goes on. The sea. And measure for measure—
Like drummers who die defending an empty drum—
Somebody picks up a puzzle and puts it together:
The gold mosaic of Byzantium.

LOOKING AT HIEROGLYPHS
IN THE BRITISH MUSEUM

Observe the thin white line of madness etched—
A slight indention, as delicate as ice.

Observe the man that William Hogarth sketched—
One eye staring stark and shadowless,
The other bleak in the eclipse of his face.

Who gave it to the observer to be God?
Some lines are curved, but other lines are straight.
Who shall then, or what high court decide
The right design?
                    The village priest is dead—
A jumble of bones in the rubble of villages.
Damp in his skull, the fables of an age
Evaporated, faded into the past,
Leaving us with the sharp-eyed psychiatrist.

Does he believe the wages of sin are death?

THE KEPT HAWK

The kept hawk that Jeffers said freedom is, is not
Hooded and sheathed, hand-fed, lashed to the gauntlet.
Its cries do not ricochet in the turbulent light—

I do not hear its terrible cry in the snow
When I go out in winter to watch the slow
Unspeakable yellowing sun descend at twilight—

Nor do I hear it at night with the owl in the thicket,
Nor does it hover over the cowardly crow,
Nor does its dark outline harrow the tyrant.

Now it perches on the wrist of Caesar,
Its black eyes blinded by the kiss of grief.
Trained to the whistle,

                    it skids to a halt in the air—
A comic character, a falling leaf
That flutters with clipped wings where it used to soar.

ROSE WINDOWS

These forms excite the eye, the spirit soars
As vaulted arch converges on a keystone.

The roses of the windows, red medallions,
Blaze in the ruby of stained-glass, blood of stars,
Glaze the eyes of saints on their stony stairs.

What slides through space to fall on holy stone—
Burns in the instant of transubstantiation,
Turns in the keyhole of unapproachable light?

The bread is bread, the wine is table wine,
But something happens in the incredible lens
These windows have become.
                                    They lay their light
Dark on the tongues of blind communicants—
Who, when they try to speak of indwelling love,
Swivel like bells in the belfries of themselves.

DUST THOU ART

"Summon all the dust to rise,
Till it stir, and rub the eyes."
—George Herbert

If thou art dust, and dust the angels are,
And dusty are the bodies of the stars
That stand in dusty stardom in the dark,

Is dust a fleshy property? Does soul
Carry its quota of dusty particle?
And what about those statues in the park
That rust in the corkscrews of their pedestals?

I like to think that star and particle
Differ only in the shape of foil—
That particles of light in dusty rooms
Shine like the stars they take their shining from.

Perhaps the dust in castle, house and home,
Is rearranged by the same busy broom
That summons all the dust when its time has come.

V.

DARKLY THROUGH A HORSEFLY'S EYE

DARKLY THROUGH A HORSE-FLY'S EYE

The horsefly's eye is curved to transmit light.
True to the hexagonal geometry
Of its molecular lattice, the horsefly's eye—
Cut and fitted for comfort and optimal sight—
Is brighter when the horsefly is in flight.

Things blur until he focuses to see
What has entered his field of clarity—
As we perceive the wrong and choose the right,
Or choose the wrong and pay the consequence,
Or do not choose, and therefore make a choice.

The horsefly has no choice. He has a lens
That closes down at death. We have a voice
That goes on speaking even after we die,
Even beyond our solid geometry.

THE BUTTERFLY

For fifteen glorious days, the butterfly
Was ablaze . . . and then its light went out,
Its twitching wings shut tightly at the last.

The bright and fragile maze of what it was
Collapsed in air, came down as dull as dust,
And blew away like scraps of nothing much.

My mind tells me a butterfly existed
Where only shards are fluttering underfoot—
Scattered bits of Mozart—tempus fugit.

Now when I see one petrified under glass,
I think how strange the uses of the past—
Especially those still hidden under ice.

At least a tree is something you can reach,
And falling leaves are something you can touch.

THE SWAN

It floated so slowly toward me in the dark,
At first I didn't recognize the swan.
It was no duck or goose—I should have known
A king had come to commandeer the park—
For when it glided closer, I saw it look
Sharply at the shadows along the shore.

No swan like this was drawn by Audubon—
Its silver wings were tarnished, sleek and black.
A vivid swan of myth in a shrinking pond
Fixed me with a penetrating look,
Rose up in its wrath and leaned as if to strike.

It seemed annoyed when I did not respond.
Its head sank back on the arches of its neck
And curved in the asking, like a question-mark.

THE UNICORN

When first I came upon the unicorn—
The sea behind it calm as wind-blown glass—
I scoffed at the pretense of its gilded horn.

But then it stamped and neighed, and I was afraid
That even apparitions—splendid beasts—
Are bred by the gods for devious purposes.

"Call the hunters, call the quivering hounds.
Yellow coronets call down the sun
To witness where a unicorn has run."

When I looked back upon where it had been,
I saw the tracks of a white and glistening horse
That leaped into the tide.
                                        The sky was black.
A lazy gull was swallowed by a cloud
That swelled to immense proportion until it died.

THE TOAD

The thing that was a toad lay in the road.

A hit-and-run, it stretched in its rubber skin
That left a track like a tire-tread, a stain
Trucks ran over until it was corrugated.

Night is a hunter. It stalks a country road,
Headlights blinding the deer—

                    and here's the spot
Jack hit a buck that leaped right through his windshield,
Bleeding to death where his wife sat,

                      thank God that
She was getting the cows in—

                    but there's the child
Who'll come upon a corrugated toad,
Who'll pick it up and take it home all stiff
And play with it, and sail it over the roof
When tired of it—

               he knows its only a toad.
Tonight he might find a rabbit in the road.

THE COURTLY STANCE OF BASHO'S BIRD OF LOVE

What moves this courtly bird to pirouette?
Aristocratic blood? Genetic chance?
It leaps aloft on outstretched wings to dance
Around the object of its exhuberance.

It takes its ease on laquered scrolls and screens.
Cast in bronze, it lifts a dainty foot.

Glazed in the icy glow of porcelain,
A dancing crane is frozen in a dance
That caused the poet Basho to complain:

How can I capture in haiku the high-flying crane
Wading long-legged in green tidal pools?

For even as a crane flies off the page,
Another crane of indeterminate age
Alights to stand on one leg, deep in thought.

THE HAWK

My heart in hiding
Stirred for a bird.
—G.M. Hopkins, "The Windhover"

A speck in the mist of morning, dark between peaks—
A hawk aloft on the heat-waves of first light
Rose and fell until it soared out of sight.

What hawk is this, serene above a lake
Of floating cloud and islands of bare rock?

I saw it clearly pause and fold in flight
Before it dove—a feathered arrow shot
From a crystal bow.
                    I saw it bend and break
Out of a cage of cloud that held it in
Before it began the beauty of its run
Up lanes of light.
              O Bird of the Abyss—
Remote and distant—yet in that instant was
Converted by wind and sun into energy
That spilled over, and flooded the sky with fire.

THREE WAYS OF GETTING TO KNOW THE MAN THAT STANDS IN SNOW

I

He stands in snow, in snow up to his eyes.
His bones are snow, and in his veins are ice
That will not flow until a warming wind
Rearranges him.
                    Perhaps he knows the cold.
Perhaps its meaning penetrates his mind,
And that is why he holds to what he has:
The coal for eyes, the hat upon his head,
The tilted stance of a comic attitude.

What is he then, this temporary man—
A figment of a child's imagination?
Is he more than winter art in season?

Perhaps he was made for something above and beyond
The white clay of winter, shaped and given lease
To stand in the sun until he is nothing again.

II

More than most dependent upon the whim
Of the sun, the hot sun that cuts him down to size,
He dies each day. He shrinks before our eyes.

And nothing we aspire means to him
What it means to us—although we share the same
Breathing space,
                                    the same procession of days,
The same uncertain balance of fire and ice.
Like the sand-castle, he is beholden to time—
And whitely rides the flow of winter-tide.

Like icicles that weep before they die,
And die because they cannot help but weep,
He weeps for what in fact he cannot keep—

Not even for a season, like other men,
Whose souls are composed of a harsher crystalline.

III

Born of snow, he "is" snow. That's all he is—
Snow to the heart like an arrow of splintered ice,
Unless he grows in the quick of your hands and becomes
Whatever you decide to make of him.

Now he stands opaque in his paradise—
In winter-white, as innocent as dove,
Waiting for your touch to give him the shape
Of something humanesque.

                             Until then, he sleeps—
As once you slept in the bland of your innocence,
Before the hand that shaped you in your sleep
Countered fate with circumstance.

                             Shall he dance
The white dance of winter? Shall he suddenly sing
About what happened to snap him out of his trance—
The sleight-of-hand that made him what he is?

VI.

NIGHTS OF WOODSMOKE

NIGHTS OF WOODSMOKE

For Eugene, back in the bayou . . .

Of course it came about here in the South:
The clapboard church minus a bell, the moss
Loose and long on black oaks, the cypress-knees
Protruding above still water, the cotton-mouth
Basking on the flattest rock on earth.

Nowhere else the rows of unpainted houses
Leaning together as bleak as black-eyed peas,
The windows curtained over with trouble and death;

Nowhere else the keen dark sounds of sorrow
Magnified by moon in a sugar-pine;

Nowhere else the syncopated line
Of blue emotion rising out of a hollow
That coughs up meaning out of the bone's marrow—
As blue as woodsmoke where the blues began.

PASSING THROUGH KANSAS

Now looking back at the bricks of a town in Kansas—
Bloodstained and dark with wheel-ruts under the snow—
Deadwood Dick was born in a town like this.
He called it home.
               And over him the grass—
Interweaving the same old roots in a soil
Worn out now, bruised and bisected by roads
Roaring off into dustbowls of empty space;

But still it coils and uncoils its tumbleweed,
Cutting it loose when the time has come to roll
Over the countryside.
               He came to grief,
The story goes, but everything came to grief:
Buzzards were busy, the bones of buffalo
Piled up like cordwood, the hides were dried in the sun,
And hunters shot down an occasional Indian.

ON A DIG IN THE BADLANDS

I found a broken wing. Was it a hawk?
I picked it up, and saw the other thing—
A bony hand, that looked like it was reaching
For a friend to help it out of the rock
It was embedded in.

                      The thing was stuck.
The others came, and carefully cut it out,
And brushed it off, and hung it on the rack
Where Michael was—the lizard-skeleton—
As long and slender, in limestone, as a leaf
The wind blew down.

                    How delicate, these bones!
Yet all is bone: the breath we have become,
The dust embedded, the names on marble tombs
That date the act—as if, in falling down,
We sleep and dream of getting up again.

TREE-CUTTING AT CHRISTMAS

Each year they came to lop the spires off,
Leaving the stumps of amputated chapels.

It wasn't Christmas yet—six weeks until—
He heard the grind of gears going up the rough
Pasture road,
                    and thought it loud enough
To send some white-tails vaulting through the brush
Or scare a mess of quail.
                              It was the truck,
Of course, the screaming saws, the clumsy rush
To cut enough trees so city-folk could stand

Beneath dry, sagging branches and admire
A glittering tree in the windows of the night.

It didn't make sense to tear up the woods each year
Just to hang lights on the limbs of a dying tree.

That night it snowed. The forest was quiet and cold.

NEAR WOUNDED KNEE, SOUTH DAKOTA

Its plummeting body profiled like an arrow,
The dark hawk dove at a swiftly moving target
Obscured by snow.

                         After the groundhog, a rabbit
Leaped out of the clutches of those retracted claws
That sprang open to strike.

                             The hawk was slow—
A fact that amused the man behind the rock
Stalking a cluster of shifting buffalo.
Hawk-like himself in the darkly falling snow,
He tested the pull on his bow and fitted an arrow—
Winging it skillfully at the back of a bull.

Pocked now with shallow graves and wallows, the

                                      unmarked
Bones of hawks and Indians,

                     this bleak plain
Rolls away empty into a gray horizon
Deathly still—as if it were waiting for something.

MOUNTAIN LION, TROY, MONTANA

The hungry lion mangled what it could reach.
It wasn't a serious loss, but it was enough
To send the cattle-ranchers out beating brush
On principle.
          They soon found traces of it:
A streak of claw on the side of a newborn calf,
Teeth marks on the broken neck of a colt.
They saw where it had dragged a deer, ate half,
The hollow it slept in, and where it lay in wait
To strike again.
            The lion watched them come—
Up a box canyon, high in the rocks where the dogs—
Howling, wolf-like huskies, had driven it.
The cat was treed, tired and lame, but it fought.
I saw it up close—the burning coals of its eyes.
It took five shots to put the fire out.

WAITING FOR WILD HORSES

The brightest green between the whitest rock
Carpets the high pastures of wild horses.

Time and space are measured by emptiness—
The sky standing on end, a turquoise lake,
Black pines in crevices, and eagles black
Against the icy peaks.
               The hours pass.
Slow parades of clouds pile up in space.
At last the herd appears.
                   The horses are back,
Led by a stallion with tawny mane that stands
Profiled on a rise—ten mares, six colts,
Kicking at their shadows—and not far behind,
A wolf at the tree-line, stalking the nearest foals.

The stallion snorts and stamps. The mares respond.
He calmly swings his herd to higher ground.

THE HANGMAN OF HANGTOWN (PLACERVILLE)

The hangman's noose is swinging in the wind.
Cut it down quickly, before the hangman comes,
Before the coil of hemp and twisted twine
Finds a human target to define.

Who is stalking the cricket in the dark?
Who the whale, under a hard harpoon?
Who the sparrow? Who the hooded hawk?

Like wind that tumbles dust-devils in its wake,
Slams the barn door, howls in the empty well,
A hangman is tracking the vast invisible.

What force is this? What face? What hourglass
Empties a gibbet, springs a trap at dawn?

The hangman is anonymous, his eyes
Glint like the windowpanes in abandoned towns.

THE DARK BROWN OWL

The dark brown owl, in slow and easy sweep,
Commands the fields awash in wheat and corn.
He flies the hilly rise and hollow seep
To find the furry mice he feeds upon—
And rabbits, too, that he contrives to catch
Before they leap.
                        The owl's enormous eyes
Oversee the countryside for miles.
And all around know who is coming by
Whenever they hear the hooting of an owl—
Or see him courting in a cabbage patch
As darkness falls.
                        The owl and I keep watch—
I within a corner of my sleep,
He where shadows coil upon the grass,
Or hang from trees to watch the hours pass.

MY DAUGHTER IS A RUNNER

—for Shauna

My daughter is a runner. She moves on wheels
Not of her own devising, more than skill.
I see this when she flows by like a Pegasus—
Heels in flight—

      or slicing the wind like an eagle,
She leaves behind her a bright, invisible trail—
As if she had, in the leaning, learned to push
Beyond the visible.

      She has become the myth
She took upon herself—transcending the female,
The daughter, the flesh.

      Her foot is a flashing hoof,
Her hair a flowing mane, her body sleek
As she goes by on the stroke of an inner clock
That strikes in her ears only.

      I see her face
Flushed, exaulted, strange—as if she had seen
What Icarus saw when he soared into the sun.

THE RARE BLACK SWAN SHOT DOWN NEAR SACRAMENTO

The sky was torn, a jagged wing-blade bent,
As down in spirals tumbled the wounded swan.

It took but a bullet to crack the crystal dawn—
The beauty of water and sky cut down in an instant.

I saw the awkward, ugly, twisted thing
Ragged and wet, limp in the mouth of the dog
That dragged it—bleeding—through a muddy bog
To the hunter's blind.
                              The shot still rings
Loud in the mind of the hunter, the sky, the swan
Spinning forever into a sullen dawn—
Echoing still, because of an intervention
Nothing can rectify.
                              How long will it take
Before the sky is empty of eagles and larks
Falling like stars, because of a shot from the dark?

WASHINGTON'S MONUMENT, 1985

Thou, Washington, art all the world's, the continents'
entire—/ not yours alone, America.
—Walt Whitman, "Washington's Monument, 1885"

This old marble, remote and monumental,
That sways in its aging stone like a leaning tower,
Will fall or soar.
                The narrow shaft of its spire
Contains within itself the Elemental—
Lift and star-thrust, the Humming Invisible.

Von Braun and Steinmetz understood the spark
That drives a man to empty his mind, to fill
Infinite space with thoughts made visible.

And Washington, upon the Delaware,
Didn't avoid the sight of those banked-fires—
Nor have the leaders after him,
                    who find
Their words and gestures recycled in other spheres—
Who do not measure their years on level ground,
But balance—poised—on a planet between stars.

VII.

SIGHTING REALITY THROUGH THE NECK OF A BOTTLE

SIGHTING REALITY THROUGH THE NECK OF A BOTTLE

When tilted toward light, another kind of world
Reflects the work of salt and a grinding sea.
The glass is etched. A bright reality
Burns in the turning at the tunnel's end.

Is this a fallen jewel of the sun in my hand?
It flares in its flaws, like the sun in the glass of Chartres.
Perhaps a message from an uncharted planet
Was bottled in space and cast into solar wind
To land where it has fallen in the sand.

Or is it only what it seems to be?
For here are the marks of the pouring,

                                        the marks of the mold,
Benchmarks of the glazier's art that seize
The smallest error, magnify each flaw,
Making a maze through which the mind can flow.

SEEING BRIGHTLY WITH THE MIND'S EYE

How many kinds of world do the blind contain?
Their hands touch infinite imaginings.

They reach out for texture, the shape of rain,
That tells by touch all manner of living thing:
The wet, the dry, the thick, the thinly laid.

Like bricks that make a wall stand where it is,
They stand too—in the bright cage of their blood
That they will never see except in shade.

And yet, in coursing praise, the mind's eye senses
The essence of what is, and what is not,
Sends the singer soaring beyond the song

Until each note transposes, magnifies
What Homer did, and those who encapsulate
The dark and light of a long, continuous night.

A SPIDER IN THE DARK

Casting its net upon the teeming air,
A spider in the dark has come to stay.

It weaves a window like a star in sky—
A resting place, a certainty in space
That pin-points time, and bridges the abyss
Between realities.
                    "O spider in the dark—"
"Is there no going back beyond the spark"
"That started it?"
                    Einstein said it was like
Stepping out lightly into a vast unknown—
Not knowing if his foot would fall on stone.

He didn't speak of the starkness of standing on air,
Reflecting on things the mind can scarcely track:
The moving sums of numbers—wings and words—
Intangible blurs, that hover like hummingbirds.

REFLECTED SUNLIGHT
IN A CLEFTED ROCK

"The sun is a hole in the sky."
—a Zuni observation

A narrow slit of high, unfolding sky
Preoccupies my waking hours and dark.
It lights the pit within the clefted rock
That locks me into my reality.

Is there a way—from where I stand—to break
The flow of mind and matter through the crack
In Plato's cave?
                        If sun is but a slit—
A bright and glassy glimpse of infinite;
If life is a key that lingers in a lock;
If I, like stone, fall free by falling back,

What measure fills the hole that still remains
To prove that it, too, had an origin?
I tell my son to turn all ways at once
Because his father never learned to dance.

OWL-CALL

The owl upon the branch is calling God.
The hollow sound of its echo, long and low,
Warns the field mouse, naked under snow,
To take a turn about the countryside.

The beak and brow that cross beneath its horns
Are carved like those of Michaelangelo's Moses—
That sullen prophet, angry in repose,
Who spoke to seven owls upon a mountain.

What's in owl-call? What did Moses find
When he went up to bargain for the world?
What's in the bowl of an owl's uncluttered mind?

The owl upon the branch is ageless, old,
And those who know the word for what it is
Listen to owls like learning another language.

LOOKING AT A ZEN PAINTING IN AN ART MUSEUM

In this scroll, a sense of things unseen.
Is it the pine, leaning over the rim
As if to summon reality by name?
Is it the hawk, falling with folded wing,
That cannot fly out of the skin of its being?
Is it the monk on the cliff's edge, with folded arms,
Who sits in the center of something holding him?

Caught like the hawk, I cannot, just by looking,
Step into time with the pine and the holy man.
They dwell on the rim of a mountain, they conjoin—
Consecrated by time before my time.

Roughed by the wind, and rinsed in a towering mist,
The two have come together in a tryst
Deep in the mind's eye, deep in the eye of the storm.

THE COLORS OF THE COUNTRY OF THE BLIND

The colors of the country of the blind
Take on status, stature. They sway in the wind,
And glitter like goldfish in a spring-fed pond.

The old man said his blindness made him young.
Nothing faded. Nothing ran down in him.
The same old colors were there—as loud and strong
As they once were when he sounded out the rhyme
Inherent in each thing.
                    From that time on,
He said, the world unfolded like a fan—
The huge, hand-painted, oriental kind,
That whispers when it closes its wings or expands.

He saw it all. The colors in his mind
Wheeled on command, collided, sent off sparks
Igniting the dark like a fountain of fireworks.

THE BLONDE BATHER OF
PROVENCE AND POMPEII

--from the painting by Auguste Renoir

Her body was his, but her eyes belonged to the sea.
He must have seen what she was seeing, when
He painted her blonde against the blue, her hair
Glistening gold and windblown. Seated that way

She looked like the girl in the fresco in Pompeii
The painter had seen reclining on a wall:
Her burnished hair a newly minted coin
Dropped by the sun, and caught in the mouth of a wave

That sealed her smile and lacquered her flesh with ashes.
Renoir must have guessed that she was the same
When he saw her smiling: the same look about her

That she was wearing later, her back to the sea—
The same sea, but twenty centuries later,
When loved and painted (perhaps) by the same painter.

SEEING WITH THE THIRD EYE

The unmistakable image of Adam's eye
Meets the eye that is staring back at me.
What is behind this quick-silver secrecy?
Who am I? Who is he? Which of us the spy?

Behind these walls are walls, and then the sky
Reflecting space as far as eye can see
And back again, into the inner me.

I am perplexed. The light within the eye
Rings my eye as if it had thrown a stone
Lightly into the pond I am inside.

What are these ripples that spread from bone to bone
Until each cell reflects another one?
Are they a part of the Adam who never died,
Who never gave up looking for the garden?

PINS AND WHEELS: A METAPHYSICAL

Do stones in the crystal chambers of their souls
Move without meaning in their molecules?
Do even the smallest, the insignificant least—
Like dust on the tusk of the most revolting beast—
Detect in the flesh of the invisible
A sense of purpose?
       If souls have knees that kneel,
And stones have brains that calculate the cost
Of energy, then even the busy flea—
Vastly underrated by the cat—
Plays a part in a delicate balancing act:
The pins and wheels that keep the world afloat.

Now when I feel the pitch and tilt of an ark
That I have been riding too lightly in the dark,
I praise the water flowing under my feet.

THE ISLAND DRAWN
FROM MEMORY

She drew an island, then she drew a boat—
The sea surrounding both, the water green.
Then she drew a tree.
                        She made it lean
Inward, islandward; it seemed to float
In its own sphere, as if it had a root
Independent of the island scene.

She was the tree: a stately palm, serene,
With elegant, tapering leaves. She was the boat
Floating off the shore. She was the sea, the waves,
The gentle motion of water against the hull.

She was the island, too, in other lives,
And sensed the meaning of each particle—
The sand above and pearl below the sea.
She drew and drew until she was all of these.

THE UNBLINKING BUDDHA
IN THE EYE OF STONE

An eye in a stone is never an empty hole.
Things slide through its slit—like wind, and water, and
                                                light—
The souls of dead druids, bats on their night journeys,
And other invisibles.
                        The eye of a stone—
When hung like a moon, or swung in a circle at dawn,
Or lined-up, like Stonehenge, in a slant of sun,
Unravels the meaning of light-rays in its lens.

The smallest stone—a mountain in the mind—
Turns dark into light, can radiate, can be
A timeless buddha, whose every thought is stone.

An eye so clear in its sense of identity
Centers itself like moonlight in a well—
Or sky in a diamond, or seaglow in a pearl,
Or that bright star in the ice of a sapphire's eye.

VIII.

SOONER OR LATER
DELICATE DEATH

SOONER OR LATER
DELICATE DEATH

"In the day, in the night, to all, to each
Sooner or later delicate death."
—Walt Whitman

Within the shell he had become, he felt
A bony thing cast up by a tender wave
To linger on the raging edge of a love
No longer his.
              The sea-grass flowed by, spilled
Around him. He watched a quick green crab, and felt
The sting of salt, and something else that moved
Imperceptibly, like a spring in that cave
His cavernous eyes had become.
                      He thought of a colt
He once saw kicking knee-high in the grass,
And pleasured himself with the memory of a kiss
So vast and distant, it was no more than mist
Surrounding dream.
               How delicate, he thought,
The flesh that clings and balances on bone
When hyacinths and lilacs turn to stone.

THE SPIDER

The spider walking across the coverlet
Did not expect to meet the hand of fate.
His body was the ultimate machine:
Head and thorax suspended from a frame
That slid along in supple, easy motion—
A work of art I thought it was a shame
To terminate.
                    And yet, with some regret,
I flattened him dead with a quick slap of the hand—
Reflecting, as I did so, what it meant
To be the killer on the killing end
Of this establishment.
                              I doubt it mattered
To the spider that I regretted his death—
Nor would he have halted to reflect
Had he caught me crossing his coverlet.

WHILE READING A BIOGRAPHY OF ROETHKE

All finite things reveal infinitude.
—Theodore Roethke, "The Far Field"

The finite things were easy to recall:
The greenhouse smell, the ferns and pebbles and moss
That lay on the surface of his syllables,
The thick accentuals of his grandmother's voice.

A child of winter, I remember well
The frosty panes of a winter's flowering glass
A small boy breathed on, made circles with his fingers,
Traced a face on, made peepholes through the ice
To watch the snowbirds hopping over the drifts.

A snowman stood like a shepherd, a broom for a staff,
And lambs were leaping in their white wool in the sun
Until they melted down—

                      and then the rain
That washed it all away, and left it green,
And watercolors on the windowpane.

STATUES

What do they have to do with the men that stood
Like Walt Whitman on street corners, flogging his verse—
Galileo burnt, or Mozart, in a hearse
Swallowed by fog in a forest not too proud
To overlay him in lime?
                          What stone shroud
Could hold what Moses was? A bust of Bach
Is only an echo of what the sculptor struck—
But not what Bach was about, not one small chord.

The sculptor is an assassin, with his knife
He hacks at stone until it resembles life,
Until they stand like statesmen against the dark—

Gesticulating, posing, as if the light
Will fall on their shoulders like an all-knowing cloak—
As if, in the making, they come to life again.

HECTOR SLAIN

"Where have they gone, those braggadocio boasts
we proudly flung upon the air at Lemos?"
—*The Iliad*

Who shall draw hot baths for Hector, slain—
Lying cold, where gray-eyed Athena made
The arm of Achilles slash downward with a sword?

It severed the chord that bound the boy to the man,
Laid him out in his shroud on bloodstained stone
The worse for wear.

What now? Where are the gods?
Where are the goat-herds, the feast, the fatted calf?
The groaning table is groaning under the weight
Of empty casks and broken promises.

How soft the outer, the inner reflecting the self
Uncomposed, unconscious of how it lives!
Glutted and stuffed with the self-indulgence of wine,
The soul cannot always cohabit with what it believes—
Nor can a wife survive as a widow forever.

ON FIELDS OF GREY REGRET

On fields of grey regret, the bodies fall—
Good men all, and younger than the grass
That paints them green and black.

How high must bone

Pile upon bone before the taste of brass
Legislates an end to the blood-letting?

The stones are red, the sky is red, the dawn.
A dead sun glints on rusty bayonets,
On bones the color of marble and broken slate.

On fields of grey regret, the bodies fall
In stony rows for no good reason at all—
And they are falling yet.

How deep? How tall?

How long must the wind rustle a dead man's hair?
My fingers itch to scratch an ancient sore.
How smooth the faces of those who go to war!

GONGORA

"Who remembers the prebendary?
Gongora is absolutely alone."
—From Lorca's lecture in Granada (1926)

When Gongora, in Cordoba, alone,
Contemplated roses in his courtyard,
Or watched the rain through leaded windowpanes,
Or heard, in solitude, a music heard
Only in the country of the courtly,

Did he know, then, toward the end, his hands
Were turning into marble? And that his eyes
Were turning back into the crystal sand
That makes a pearl a miracle?
                                                    Perhaps.
God knows he died without a jewel, without
The common courtesy of bread, or cape,
Or carriages to carry him about—
But bells remember and carve his name in sound:
Gongora, Gongora, loud on the cobblestones.

CHANCE ENCOUNTER
IN A CATACOMB

His hollow eyes are circles in the dark.
Deep and wide, they ignore the earth.

What did he see when the high-voltage shock
Of death and rebirth gave him back his breath?
What did he say?
                    I hold his discarded skull
And wonder at the lines and crevices
Criss-crossing the bone.
                        Should this empty bowl
That held the shapely fruit of what he was
Lie like a pottery shard on a crowded shelf?

Or did he take his pride with him, the self
That matters most when the curtain is drawn
Tightly across the eyes, the grinning mouth
That has nothing to tell us, and nothing to tell with?

Later, I was glad for the glare of the sun.

GRASS

Something moved, is moving in the grass.
I trace a shape by how the grass is bent—
The way it presses and releases prints.

What is passing? Is it wind? The grass
Senses, blade by blade, the seasons spent
Responding to rain.

                      Clump by clump, it measures
The tense duration of sun upon its face—
And what it means to fallow, green with grace,
Heavy with the wet of its well-being.

When something moves in cadence, like the wind,
And when that moving something leaves a dent,
Grass doesn't ask why it is being bent.
For grass takes root, and is easy in the space
That also is its final resting place.

IX.

THE MAN WHO WENT BEYOND E=MC2

THE MAN WHO WENT BEYOND E=MC2

Nailed to the hub of a wheel that spun him around,
The astronaut revolved at a different rate
Than Einstein calculated: the speed of light
Had nothing to do with Time in the figure-ground
Of where he was.
                    They tried to understand
How this man could transubstantiate—
Square the expanding circle of their thought,
Explicate dark passages to heights beyond
Their own imaginings,
                            as when they found
Nobody could confound him in the Sanhedrin—
And that two decades back, when a mere child
Parried question with question, as if the world
Held no terrors compared to that alien land
He knew like a native, knew like the back of his hand.

THE LAST PIETA

Hovering over her dead son like a hawk,
She fixed her eyes on the glint of a faraway thread
That only she could see.

                         He lay sprawled out,
Limp as a shawl on her knees, his head laid back,
His tangled and matted hair trailing off into dark.

He lies like this in Florence, Madrid, Milan—
Hewn by an old Michelangelo out of rock,
His hands intense on the stone as Mary's were
When she slid back the lid of the rock and found
An empty sepulchre:

                     "Where is my son?"
Find him quickly, before she averts her eyes,
Before she clips the fragile, unbroken thread
Stitching up the living and the dead,
Before she unravels the rags we inherited.

THE KEY

They always bury it deep in the stony deep
To silence it—even a bird will sing.
A master key that unlocks anything,
Anything at all—the sky, the castle, the keep—
Cannot be kept.
               For this key will not sleep,
Cannot be counted on to close its eyes,
Or look the other way, or fall on its knees
When the king goes by.
                   They say not even the Pope
Has such a key—although he carries a cloak
That makes him invisible, that glows in the dark
When darkness falls.
                 And Pilate, tall and pale,
Threw it away when it began to speak
In parables, when it began to tell
The riddle of locking and unlocking the dark.

THE DANCING ANT

The ant that is prancing on the village green
Has been accused of not assuming the stance
Of other ants.
                        Delicate of foot, he dances
With a lilting grace across the lawn.
He pirouettes in place, and darts, and runs
With a grand abandon through the grass.

The other ants judgmentally assess
Antics unseemly to an antly station.
With quick antenna quivering, they chase
The deviant from blade to shiny blade.

I have watched them cultivate their plantations.
As big as God, I stood there casting shade
Over an anthill, where a dancing ant
Was trampled under the feet of a chanting tribe.

THE HANDS THAT HELD

The hands that held the host at supper were
Bolted down not many hours after.

Were these hands more than hands? They cast a spell.
And when the hands were folded, they were still.

The fingers fondled the bread—as pliable
As clay—a sculptor's fingers, shapely, strong,
The fingers of a surgeon—

                                    or is it wrong
To speak of bread as if it were somebody's flesh—
A living thing to be molded, dissected, enmeshed in—
As if it were a thought drawn taut—a string—
Binding violinist to the violin.

They knew what it meant to be broken in the bone—
The hands bloated and torn from hanging on—
Until, at the end, they became blunt instruments.

CHRIST AND YEATS
AMONG THE VIOLETS

There you were, in the city of the sick—
Padded carpets, trolleys on rubber wheels—
A nun among the violets, the click
Of elevators punctuating your vowels
As you recited Yeats, and Crazy Jane,

And I, the Bishop, nodding over the verse,
Pretended to be affected by the lines.
But I was more affected by your voice—
The subtle arabesquing of your eyes,
The love-lines of your mouth.
                              And that was when
I realized what Yeats meant: Incongruous.
Blasphemous. Tragic. Sad. And Christ on the cross,
Who did not bleed so you could become his bride,
Sagged on his nails and quietly expired.

THIS LITTLE MAN

How Sweet and Clean are Thy Returns, O Lord.
—George Herbert

Rude, complaining, lump of ingratitude
Made out of mud that dries, at the end, to dust,
This little man—
                    unkind, distorted, lewd—
Does what he does mostly because he must,
Not because he was made for the love of God
Or for the good of us.
                    And yet he thrives—
Somehow clinging to the slender vine
That carries the animal kingdom,
                              that breeds and cleaves,
Sustaining birth beyond the shallow grave,
Beyond the span of allotted years, until
He drops like a penny into a wishing well.

Was it for the sake of a few that he came
To open gates that lead into a garden—
Or did he do it for even this little man?

THE BAT

Not too far from a goat-god in despair,
He hovered like a bat, wings whispering.

"What time is it?" A soldier muttered,
As if it mattered to anyone the hour—
Or who died when—

                              as, whetted in vinegar,
A damp sponge lay in the dust, the soldiers throwing
Dice for blood-stained linen, the women weeping.

The bat was stirring now. His wings made a whirr
Whenever he shifted from crosspiece to crosspiece to sit
Directly over the hanging head of the ghost—
That wasted body, gray and motionless.

He had him now. He thought he did. The proof
Was in that final scream before he expired.
Still, the bat was nervous. He brooded about it.

FROM A REPORT TO
THE COMMISSAR

There must be a better way of saying it:
The figure out of the ground it's embedded in—
Prematurely buried, has arisen . . .
That doesn't mean a thing to me, not that.

Get it right the first time. Spell it out.
What figure? What ground? It sounds like science fiction.
Did you see this thing they say has arisen?
Go look at it. Write a complete report.

I hope to God it's only another Christian!
This time we'll chain it and drop it into a pit
Before it becomes a god, or a fish, or corn,
And cover the spot.
                        They'll try to get it out.
They can't stand silences. They can't cope with the sound.
They'll try to roll back the rock that covers its mouth.

SUMMA

He wrote it first on Adam's back, then Eve's,
Then on the back of the snake in the slithering dark.
He nailed it down on the deck of Noah's ark
And chiselled it in stone on Jonah's grave.

Always a finger was moving over the sky
As if to show the living where to look,
As if the dark of dying was too stark,
The glassy stare too much for the naked eye.

Even his first-born slanted what he said—
Translated the sun into another tongue
That spoke of it more gently than he could.

Is this the story, darkly, or is it the blood
That dictates what is living and what is dead
And what is merely waiting for the word?

X.

GALAXIES

GALAXIES

I think of galaxies now in the brain's marrow—
Minute apostrophes that register pain,
Sorrow, and other things that move within the bone.

I think of planets within the cells that flow—
The shapes of their changing character, and how—
In the last analysis—their needs are plain:
Dolphins in a running tide, or field sparrows,
Or dark-eyed children standing in the snow.

I think of that vast, invisible terrain
Peopled by the brain's imagination
That moves in me, and flows in the same skull
I co-inhabit with the intangible.

I think of black umbrellas in the rain,
And butterflies that flutter in the sun.

MODERN ART IN SILOS
WHERE MISSILES ARE

The fingers of a surgeon, or violinist,
Dance on the keys of a computer screen.

Look at him! They said. When he was born,
No one predicted that he would co-exist
With sudden death,

                     or be the kind of artist
Whose delicate fingers, quick with a complex code,
Could make a world light up on a flashing board.

That's what he does. He keeps track of the beast
Whose eyes are flickering red and blue and green
Across the jungle of a computer screen.

He knows what it means when the killing board ignites—
Bells ringing, the missiles standing alert—

As swinging across his screen, an alien
Threatens to turn his daylight into dust.

THE VISITORS

*The whole of the Iliad lies under the shadow
of the greatest calamity the human race can
experience—the destruction of a city.*
—Simone Weil, "The Poem of Force"

With lights flashing, the spinning circular
Arrived at the sullen brink of the last hour.
Smoke was still rising, haze obliterated
What was left of the cities under fire.

Too late at the last for prayers, sackcloth, ashes,
The stunned survivors—huddled together in shock—
Watched the dark-eyed strangers disembark,
Stood impassive, pale, in clusters and rows.

The strangers strode, imposing, through the crowd.
They did not speak of God, or the spilled blood—
Slippery on the boulevard—nor did they pause
To castigate the city officials assembled.

There was nothing to say. All had been said.
Words could no longer convey the immensity.

EZEKIEL ARTICULATES HIS VISION

The wheel that curled in a candle-flame and curved
Back upon itself in a twist of smoke,
Evaporated—a shriven moth—but the wick
Burned calmly on.

              At dawn, the sunlight wove
Bright patterns laid upon a darker weave.
Ezekiel flung the curtains back, and the dark
Slid back between the pages of his book
Spread-eagled to Genesis.

              Wave upon wave,
He rode the ark of doubt. His faith was shaken.
Now he was left with the burning aftermath
Of revelation, the shock of an indrawn breath
Searing and sulphurous.

              Was he mistaken?
Did those hovering wheels appear in dream
Or were they high-priests, down from another kingdom?

EINSTEIN IN HIS STUDY, 1921

A changing point of light, not quite a star,
Flared out of sight in a corner of his eye.
It bent and blurred the plane geometry
That he was taught when things were what they were.

He thought it was a grace-note, nothing more—
A meteor, fresh-fallen into a sea
That churned in its turning at the point of entry.
Or was it, looking back, a prophecy—
The broken light of a beacon from afar?

This century broods upon catastrophe.
It knows the spark that hovered over the ark
When thunder struck, and lightning threaded the rain.
It knows the cold, kaleidoscopic eye
That Einstein caught boring through solid rock.

SYNCHRONICITY

*The dragonfly, in its present form, has existed
on this planet 300 million years.*
—Science News

Reading a book about fossils a billion years old,
I watched a bluebird build its fragile nest
In the fork of a willow.
                                        Hours passed.
It hustled about with twigs and grass and mud,
Carefully pressing each tidbit in place with a shrewd
Economy.
                        Nothing, it seems, is lost—
Not even algae, encased in volcanic glass—
Instant fossils that froze when the planet cooled.

Not even bluebirds, their tiny wings compressed
With twigs and grass and mud in that rocky place
Where birds are frozen forever, like photographs.

I turned a page. A dinosaur leaped out.
In that same instant, a dragonfly alighted
So close in time and space I could almost touch it.

FIGURINES

The sculpture in this cave is like no other:
The carved interiors, the feldspar mouth
Opening out from a concourse in the earth

Tenebrous now, as if a meteor
Solidified within another sphere
The shape of its own fire, and then gave birth
To figurines.
                  Is death or life defined here?
Stalagmites rearing up from the lava floor
Stalactites dripping, crystallites being born,
Illustrate in the frozen stone of its womb
Dendritic figures—an art that echoes art.

Yet the slow water and still out of which they arise
Might, in the making, form galaxies of glass—
Coruscate time, crystallize fire and ice.

THAT STAR

Where is that star we steer by, that shaft of light
Cold in the lens but tender in the heart?

And if it has drifted, has it drifted far
From where it flared upon the calendar?

The wise men said it was a star in fact—
And not a question mark, as when they asked

What searchlight probed the sky, what burning bright
Caught fire in the straw of prophecy.

Perhaps one night that star will reappear,
Cast fire down, consolidate its light.

Some say it will come to overpower the sky
Or lie in wait,
                                   with wise and open eye—
As if, in being, it were enough to be
A pinpoint on a vast periphery.

STARMEN

Down the feathered highways of heron and crane,
The starmen glide in their smooth conveyances.

Black against moon, and silver under the sun,
They slide through sky with a swift and easy grace
That looks like a trick of light against the dark.

What moves these men in their mysterious purpose?
Why do they ride the air in steady flow
Going somewhere not given us to know?

They seem to hover watchful, but do not speak—
As if we cannot give them what they seek,
As if their eyes are seeking other sights
That only gods can see.
                              We track their flight
With instruments designed for a lesser task,
Not even knowing the names of what we ask.

DEATH SQUARED

If death is squared with the shape and speed of light,
Can it be equated with other things in space?
If years are measured by incandescent flight,
What hour is this?

               Perhaps some other place
Looks like this, like earth, but is out of focus—
Impingeing with pale prints, subliminal traces—
Like mountains that fall upon the valley floor
And flower there, and flower in the sea,
As if the fact of falling doesn't matter
To immortality.

               The twisted tree—
Gnarled in its rock, and garlanded in air—
Does it give thought to the kind of fruit it bears?
And where is death, when sour apples fall
From dizzy heights to sweeter ports of call?

INDEX TO TITLES

INDEX TO FIRST LINES

DAVID GEORGE AND JEAN MIGRENNE,

French translator of (mostly American) poetry who, together with his friend and colleague Edouard Malka, contributed to the Spanish translation of 14 sonnets on Manolito, the Flamenco *cantaor* of Alcalá de Guadaira, published by Steve Kahn :

- *The Flamenco Project, Una ventana a la visión extranjera*, 1960-1985, Sevilla, Cajasol, 2010.

French translations:

- The 'Flamenco sonnets' (translated into French) are currently published online, as *Un Américain à Séville*, https://www.recoursaupoeme.fr/ by instalments, as of October 2018: #188, 191, 193, 195, 197 (July 2019) &c. In addition to # 188: the sonnets on Salvator Dali's Matador: *The Hallucinogenic Toreador.*

The first translation of David George's ekphrastic sonnets (on Grant Wood's *American Gothic*) was published in

- *Europe* #966, October 2009, under the title *Austere Amerique.*
- also in *Europe* #1005-1006, January-February 2013. 7 sonnets on Edward Hopper's paintings : *Railroad*

Sunset, Office in a Small City, The Barber Shop, New York Movie, Hotel Window.

Also in 4 issues of the now defunct *Frisson Esthétique* poetry magazine:

- #8, November 2009, 3 sonnets: *The Sun isolder...*; Utrillo's *Rue de Banlieue*; Van Gogh's *Sous la treille au Moulin de la Galette.*
- #12, Autumn/winter 2011/2012, 3 sonnets: *Goya's Diptych of May, 1808.*
- #13, Spring/Summer 2012, 5 sonnets: Joseph Stella's *Brooklyn Bridge.*
- #14, Spring/Summer 2013, *La Juerga* (from *The Flamenco Guitar*); 3 flamenco Sonnets (Easter week in Sevilla); 3 sonnets on Chagall (*Fiddler on the Roof and The Cello player*).

In *Peut-être*

- # 3, 2012, 4 sonnets: *Silber's Pharmacy* (Edward Hopper's *Drugstore*) and *The Sign of the Flying Red Horse* (Edward Hopper's *Gas*).

Online in *Temporel*

- #12, April 2013, 3 sonnets (Chagall's *Hommage à Apollinaire*).

- #13, September 2013, 12 sonnets. A repeat of *American Gothic;* and, inspired by Hopper: *Burly Cobb's Barn; House by the Railroad; High Noon; Compartment C, Car 293; Manhattan Bridge Loop.*

ABOUT THE AUTHOR

Widely published in Europe and America, David spent 25 years in Western Europe, Africa and the Middle East, domiciled mostly in Spain, but also in Morocco, Egypt and Turkey.

A US Army veteran of the Cold War era, he served as a member of the Counter-Intelligence Corps in Germany and Austria, plus duty in Asia and Washington, D.C.

He lectured at various European and American universities on art and anthropology, and exhibited paintings and photographs in London, Munich, Madrid, Venice and elsewhere.

An award-winning poet and prolific writer, David George's work has been published in over one hundred literary magazines and anthologies, including The Anthology of Magazine Verse and The Yearbook of American Poetry. He is the author of *Things of the Sea Belong to the Sea*, a collection of his sea poetry. David has written more than 6,000 sonnets and several books are in different stages of publication.

He received the Sacramento Metropolitan Art Commission's Works in Performance Award plus publication of his book *Lamentation for Emmanuel* (Wooden Angel Press). His book on gypsies and asuntos gitanos, *The Flamenco Guitar* (Society of Spanish Studies) was one of the many products of his years living among the gypsies in Andalucia, and is widely regarded as a ground-breaking work in what was at the time a non-existent field.

Printed in the United States
By Bookmasters